The ABC's of Edisto

A.E. Inabinet

By

A.E. Inabinet

2019

Dedicated to Taylor, love you always and forever

There is a little place we really love to go. This place is called Edisto. Here is a little bit you really ought to know.

A is for Atlantic Ocean. Our neighbor on one side. Always be a good neighbor and help keep it clean.

B is for Botany Bay. Go explore its driftwood beach covered in shells, old brick and more. Just make sure to visit at low tide to see all its glory glow.

C is for crab. They are fun to watch scurry along the shore. But it is best for you to stay away and let them make their way. (They can be a little crabby.)

D is for digging in the sand. Oh, the fun you will have. But when you are done, have some more fun and fill the holes back up.

E is for the Edisto Bookstore. There are plenty of books and much more for you to check out. Please be sure to say hello to Emily Grace, the resident cat, who works there at the store.

F is for fishing in the creeks or from the beach. Who knows what you will catch? Spot tail? Trout? Bet you can't wait to find out.

G is for gulls looking for a snack. You will see these friends walking on the beach or flying all about. Hi there, gull.

H is for history. Edisto is full of that.
We have a museum where you can learn
all about our past.

I is for islands since we are not just one, but three. There is Little Edisto Island, Edisto Island and Edisto Beach.

J is for Jungle Road. Please tell your Mom and Dad to take it slow. It's 30mph just so they know.

K is for kites flying high up in the sky. Get a running start and watch it take flight. Be sure to hold on tight.

L is for lights out for sea turtles. Please ask your Mom and Dad to find out more and help our turtles out. Thank you from our sea turtles.

M is for the mystery tree you will see in the creek not too far from Edisto Beach. It's decorated for each holiday and season. The mystery is who its decorator might be.

N is for the nests marked along the shore. This is where our sea turtles are born.

O is for oysters that are so yummy to eat. Just don't step on them in the creeks. They will hurt your little feet.

P is for Palmetto State also known as South Carolina. This is where Edisto can be found. If you are here, enjoy your stay and come back again someday. If you are away, we hope you will join us for a stay.

Q is for quahog, but you can call me a clam. Thank goodness for me cause things that start with Q are hard to be found.

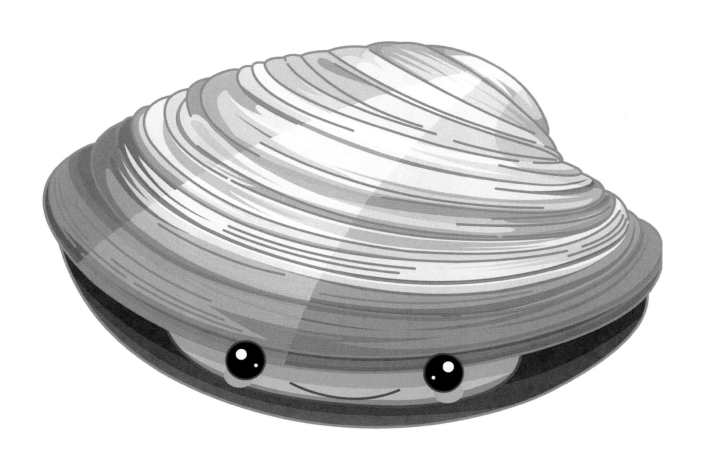

R is for riding bikes all over our little town. There are bike paths to help you get around.

S is for the serpentarium filled with snakes, alligators and more. S is also for our state park with its learning center and trails to explore.

T is for the tide that ebbs and flows. Sometimes it's high and sometimes it's low. Just see the picture below.

OCEAN TIDES

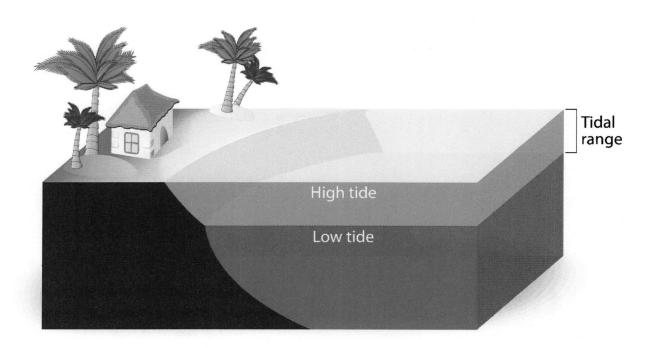

U is for umbrellas all along the shore. Folks put them there to protect them from the sun's glow.

V is for a vacation the whole family can enjoy. Family friendly vacation spot is what we are known for.

W is for waves splashing on the shore. The sound may make your Daddy snore. They are also fun for riding or floating up and down.

X is for x marks the spot we like to go.

It is a treasure to be found for sure.

We call it Ed-e-sto just so you know.

Y is for yellow polka dot bikini. See if you can spot one on the beach.

Z is for zipping to Edisto as fast as you can making new friends along the way and while you play.

Hope you enjoyed my little book. Thank you for your support and to everyone who encouraged me to go on this adventure.

Blessings and positive vibes,

A.E. Inabinet

Made in the USA
Monee, IL
27 October 2020